NATURE WALK

by Douglas Florian

Greenwillow Books New York

Crayons and a black pen
were used for the full-color art.
The text type is Cheltenham.

Library of Congress Cataloging-in-Publication Data

Florian, Douglas.
Nature walk / Douglas Florian.
p.   cm.
Summary: Two children walk through the woods with a guide,
exploring trails and observing nature around them.
ISBN 0-688-08266-1.   ISBN 0-688-08269-6 (lib. bdg.)
1. Nature—Pictorial works—Juvenile literature.
[1. Nature.]   I. Title.
QH46.F66   1989   508.315'2—dc19
88-39430   CIP   AC

TO MY DAUGHTER NAOMI

TRAIL
BEGINS

On the trail.

Cottontail.

Bluejay.

8

Fly away.

Stepping stones.

14

Pinecones.

Hidden lake.

Lunch break.

Rotting log.

21

Bullfrog.

Back on the trail.

Swallowtail.

Ant mound.

Homeward bound.

Can you find these?

Eastern Cottontail

Harebells

Bluets

Spotted Tiger Moth

Birch Tree

Vole

Beaver

Red-headed
Woodpecker

Shrew

Gray Squirrel

Loon

Wood Turtle

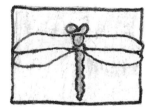

Dragonfly

Shooting Star

Bluebird

Giant Hornet

Rosy Maple
Moth

Trillium

White-tailed
Deer

Deer Mouse

JP
Florian, Douglas.
Nature walk $12.95